Add...

PETER PATILLA

KINGFISHER BOOKS

Kingfisher Books, Grisewood & Dempsey Ltd,
Elsley House, 24–30 Great Titchfield Street,
London W1P7AD

First published in 1990 by Kingfisher Books

Reprinted 1990

BRITISH LIBRARY CATALOGUING IN PUBLICATION DATA
Patilla, Peter
Good adding.
1. Arithmetic. Addition
I. Title   II. McKenna, Terry   III. Series
513′.2

ISBN 0-86272-517-8

Editor: John Grisewood

Illustrations: Terry McKenna
Design: Robert Wheeler Design Associates

Phototypeset by Southern Positives and Negatives (SPAN),
Lingfield, Surrey

Printed in Spain

Contents

♦ Adding with small numbers
page 4

♠ Adding with grids
page 14

♣ Adding with money
page 24

♠ Adding games
page 6

♣ Addition problems
page 16

♥ Adding with measures
page 26

♣ Investigating addition
page 8

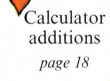
♥ Calculator additions
page 18

♦ Adding and data handling
page 28

♥ Addition puzzles
page 10

♦ Missing numbers in additions
page 20

♠ Glossary
page 29

♦ Adding larger numbers
page 12

♠ Number pattern in additions
page 22

♣ Answers
page 30

Index
page 32

Adding with small numbers

Magic squares

It is thought that magic squares were first discovered about 2200 BC in ancient China by Emperor Yu. They were called Loh-Shu and dot patterns were used instead of numbers.

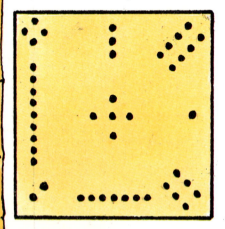

A Loh-Shu
It is 'magic' because the number of dots in each line, column and diagonal is the same.

LOH·SHU

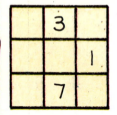

Can you complete these magic squares? Each row, column and diagonal must total 15.

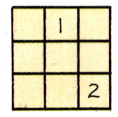

Totalling scores

Adding the numbers you score in games is an important skill. Can you find this score by adding the numbers in your head?

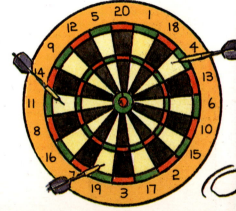

4

Addition walls

Look closely at this addition wall.
Can you see how the number
on the top brick is found?

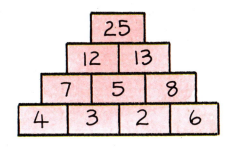

Copy and complete these addition walls.
One of the walls has lots of possible answers.

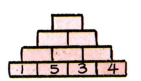
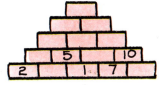
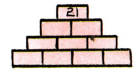

Adding digits investigation

Here are all the ten possible digits:

You can use some of these digits to investigate number problems.

Choose these four
digit cards.

Make totals from the cards.
You can only use + and =.
Here are some totals.

$4 + 5 = 9$ $4 + 2 + 7 = 13$ $5 + 2 + 7 + 4 = 18$

Can you find some more?

Choose four digit cards yourself.
Investigate the totals you can make.

Adding games

Patience game: Make Twenty

Use a pack of playing cards with all the picture cards taken out.

Shuffle the pack and put it face down on the table.
Turn over one card at a time and place it face up in line.

This set totals 20.

When you see a set of 'consecutive' cards which totals 20 gather the set up and close any gaps.
A set can have as many cards in it as you want but the total of the set must be 20.
Try to end up with as few cards in the line as you can.

Twenty-one game

A game for two players.
Use a set of digit cards 1–9.

Toss to see who goes first.
Take turns to choose a digit card and place it in the centre of the table. The total of this set of cards in the centre is important.
The aim of the game is either to make the total exactly 21 or to make your opponent go over 21.
If you total 21 score one point.
If you go over 21 score zero points.
Play several rounds to decide the winner.

Cover-up game

There is a popular dice game which uses simple adding although some skill is needed when the game is being played.

Several players can take part.
The first player rolls two dice and finds the total.
One or more numbers are then covered which match the total.

For example 8 may be used to cover

Only one dice is rolled when the remaining numbers total less than 6.
The turn ends when no more numbers can be covered up by the dice total.

The winner is the one who covers up all the numbers or who has the lowest total uncovered at the end.

Joining dots game

Lots and lots of people play joining the dots game to pass the time away.
Two dots are joined by a straight line.
Whoever can complete a square writes their initial inside the square.
The player who completes most squares is the winner.

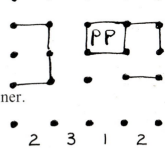

More skill can be added to this game by putting numbers inside the dots.
The game is played as usual with each player trying to complete as many squares as possible.
When all the squares are complete each player totals the numbers in their squares.
The winner is the player with the highest total.

Investigating addition

When trying some of these investigations remember that there are lots of different answers to some of the problems. It is important to set your work out neatly so that other people can see what you have been doing.

Consecutive sums

Here are some sets of consecutive numbers and their sums.

$$1 + 2 + 3 + 4 \boxed{\text{SUM}} \!\!\!> 10$$
$$11 + 12 + 13 \boxed{\text{SUM}} \!\!\!> 36$$
$$8 + 9 \boxed{\text{SUM}} \!\!\!> 17$$

Try and find sums, up to 50, which you can make by adding two consecutive numbers.

Which sums can you make by adding three consecutive numbers?

Are there any sums you cannot make by adding consecutive numbers?

Square number totals

Use a set of number cards 1–10.
Put the cards into pairs.
Each pair must add up to a 'square number'.

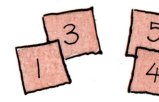

Here are some square numbers:

   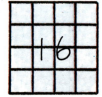

How many pairs of cards can you find?

Try making sets of three cards which add up to square numbers.

Adding light bars

Use a calculator.
Add up the light bars which make the numbers.

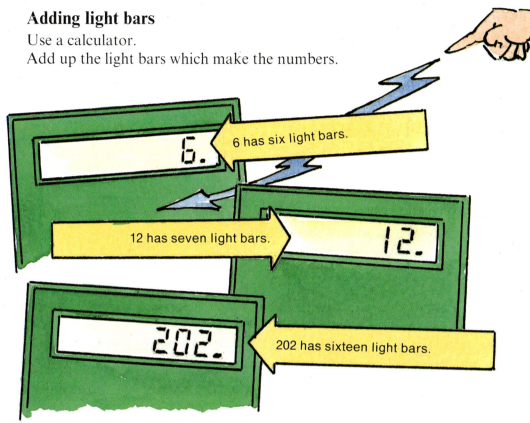

6 has six light bars.

12 has seven light bars.

202 has sixteen light bars.

How many different numbers can you make which have eight light bars?

Explore different numbers of light bars.

Dice totals

Use one dice.
Roll the dice several times.
Investigate which number is most likely to turn up.

Use two dice.
Roll them and find the total.
Investigate which total is most likely to turn up.

Addition puzzles

Your addition skills can help you solve puzzles.

Alphabet codes

Find the answers to the sums.
Use the answer code to find the letters.
Then, rearrange the letters to find the name of a country.

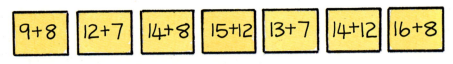

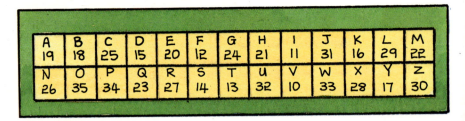

A	B	C	D	E	F	G	H	I	J	K	L	M
19	18	25	15	20	12	24	21	11	31	16	29	22

N	O	P	Q	R	S	T	U	V	W	X	Y	Z
26	35	34	23	27	14	13	32	10	33	28	17	30

What is the name of the country?
Make up some alphabet codes of your own.

Word sum puzzles

In this sum each letter stands for a number.
The letter D = 5.
Can you find what the other letters stand for?

```
  CAN
+ ADD
-----
GOOD
```

Now try this
Word Sum Puzzle.

The letter O = 9

```
 LOST
+  IT
-----
LOOK
```

10

Addition square puzzles

Which numbers go in the
empty squares?
The horizontal sums must
be correct.
The vertical sums must be
correct.

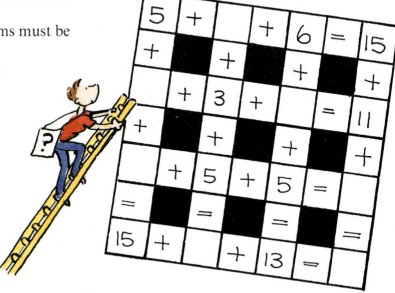

Word total puzzles

Each letter of the alphabet can have a value.

A	B	C	D	E	F	G	H	I	J	K	L	M	N	O	P	Q	R	S	T	U	V	W	X	Y	Z
1	2	3	4	5	6	7	8	9	10	11	12	13	14	15	16	17	18	19	20	21	22	23	24	25	26

ANT is worth $1 + 14 + 20 = 35$

ZEBRA is worth $26 + 5 + 2 + 18 + 1 = 52$

Can you find an animal worth less than ANT?
Can you find an animal worth more than ZEBRA?

Adding larger numbers

How good are you at adding 2-digit numbers?

Euler's square

In the 18th century a Swiss mathematician called Leonard Euler
created this special square.

All the numbers from 1 to 64 appear in the square.

What is special about the totals in:

> each row?
> each column?
> each of the four squares?

Explore other totals in Euler's special square.

How good are you at adding 3-digit numbers?

Consecutive numbers
Pairs of consecutive 3-digit numbers have been added together to make these totals.

Can you find the pairs of numbers?

Dice game

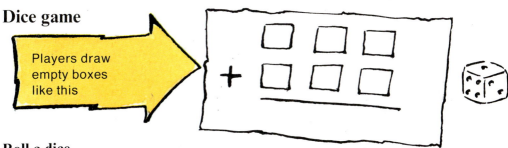

Players draw empty boxes like this

Roll a dice
Each player writes the number rolled in any of the boxes
(do not let the other players see where you put the numbers!)
Roll the dice again and put the number in another box.
Keep doing this until all the six boxes are full.
Each player finds the total of their sum.
The person with the total nearest to 500 wins.
Play several games.

All digit adds
Each of these sums uses all the digits 1–9.

654	586	216
+ 318	+ 341	+ 738
972	927	954

Can you find some sums of your own which use all the digits 1–9?
This is quite a challenge!

Adding with grids

Addition grids

Here is a simple addition grid.
Can you see how it works?

+	3	6	8
2	5	8	10
5	8	11	13
7	10	13	15

+	5		9	
2	7		11	13
	9			
			18	
10	15	17		
			21	

Here is an addition grid with some numbers missing. Copy it and find the missing numbers.

Problem grids

Some grids make you think!

The total of each row is shown.
The total of each column is shown.
What could the numbers
in the grid be?

7

5

8 4

There may be more than one answer.

Triangle grids

Grids do not have to be made from squares.

Here is a grid made from triangles.
The numbers 1–8 are missing from the grid.
When a pair of numbers touch their total
must be ODD.
Numbers do not touch at corners only on sides.
Copy the grid and try to find where to put
the numbers. There are several possible answers.

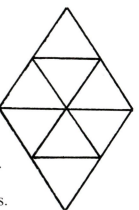

Digit grids

Grids which have lots of digits in them can be used for making up
problems. Here is a chain of digits which add up to 20.

4	8	7	2	9	1	3	1
1	②	④	9	5	3	5	6
7	2	③	①	⑤	④	3	5
1	8	7	6	1	①	5	6
4	3	1	2	6	2	4	3
1	2	9	3	4	1	2	1
3	3	4	8	5	3	6	4
2	5	2	7	9	4	8	2

Can you find any more 20 chains?
What is the longest 20 chain you can find?

Choose a different total and explore chains which
make your total.

Addition problems

Addition problems come in all shapes and sizes. Some problems are simple and straightforward, others are there to make you think. See how you get on with these problems.

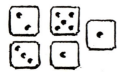

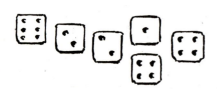

Dice problem

Look carefully at these pictures of dice. Some of the dice spots are touching the table.
Can you find out how many spots touch the table in each set of dice?
It will help if you examine how a dice is numbered.

Word problem

I have 148 stamps from America,
276 from Spain
and 236 from France.
How many stamps
do I have altogether?

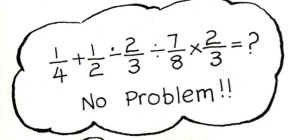

$$\frac{1}{4} + \frac{1}{2} - \frac{2}{3} \div \frac{7}{8} \times \frac{2}{3} = ?$$
No Problem!!

Mental problems

What do two quarters add up to?
What is half add a quarter?
What do two halves make?

Digit problems

Use the digits 1–9.
The middle number is odd.
Each pair of numbers has an odd total.
The five vertical numbers have an odd total.
The five horizontal numbers have an odd total.
PROBLEM: Where do the numbers 1–9 go?

Calculator problems

How many days has it been since your fifth birthday?

How many days have passed since you were born?

How many drinks do you think you have in one year?

Real problems

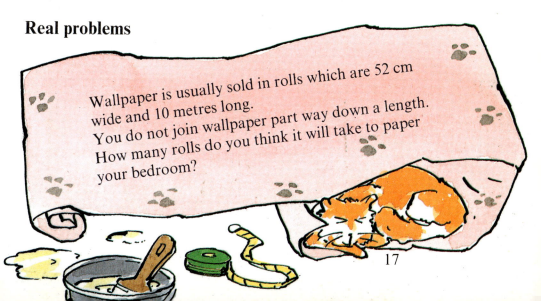

Wallpaper is usually sold in rolls which are 52 cm wide and 10 metres long.
You do not join wallpaper part way down a length.
How many rolls do you think it will take to paper your bedroom?

17

Calculator Additions

A calculator can be used to help you add up large numbers. It can also be used to explore and experiment with addition of numbers.

Limited touches

The keys must be touched SIX times, no more, no less.

Here are two ways an answer of 20 can be made with SIX touches.

$8 + 9 + 3 =$

$1 \; 0 + 1 \; 0 =$

Can you find some more ways of making 20 with SIX touches?
Now try and make 20 with FIVE touches.

Target

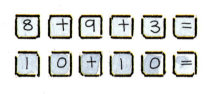

You can only touch these keys

Each key can be touched as often as you like.
They can be touched in any order.
Not all of them have to be touched.

13 can be made like this

$3 + 3 + 7 =$

17 can be made like this

$7 + 4 + 3 + 3 =$

Try to make as many numbers between 10 and 30 as you can.

Forbidden key

You are NOT allowed to touch the 8 key.
Here are two ways of finding the answer to $18 + 6$ without touching the 8 key.

$17 + 1 + 6 =$ $\cdot 9 + 9 + 6 =$

Try to find different ways of doing these sums without touching the 8 key.

$48 + 3$ $28 + 8$ $84 + 16$ $88 + 8$

ZAP the digit

A game for two players.

Put a large number on the display.

To ZAP a digit means to replace it with a zero by doing an addition sum. Each player takes turns to choose a digit to ZAP.

You can ZAP 4 by adding 600.
The 4 becomes zero.

You can ZAP 3 by adding 70.
The 3 becomes zero.

Who will make the last ZAP?

Missing numbers in additions

Some algebra work is concerned with finding 'missing numbers'.
The missing numbers can be in EQUATIONS, in SUMS, in
PROBLEMS. Try to find the missing numbers in the following
activities.

Simple equations

Each of these equations has a missing number.
There is only one possible answer to each equation.

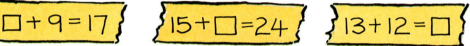

Open equations

Sometimes equations can have several possible answers.

There are two missing numbers in each of these equations.
How many pairs of numbers can you find for each equation to
make it true?

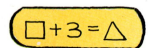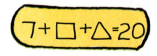

Addition sums

Each star stands for a missing digit.
Use your addition skills to work out which digit each star
stands for.

```
    43          *6          38
  + 2*        + 98        + **
  ----        ----        ----
   *1         *5*          66
```

Addition grids

Some numbers are missing from the outside of this addition grid.
What could the numbers be?
Is there only one possible answer?

+		
	7	8
	10	11

Word problems

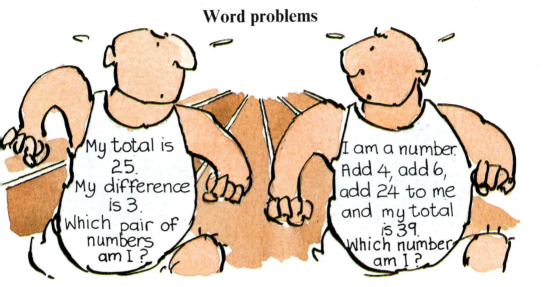

My total is 25.
My difference is 3.
Which pair of numbers am I?

I am a number.
Add 4, add 6, add 24 to me and my total is 39.
Which number am I?

Addition sequences

Find the missing numbers in these addition sequences.

45 50 ** 60 ** 70 ** 80

34 ** 42 46 ** ** 58 **

** ** 44 51 58 ** ** **

Missing fractions

Find the missing fractions.

$\frac{1}{2} + \square = \frac{3}{4}$ $\frac{1}{4} + \square = 1$ $\frac{3}{4} + \square = 1\frac{1}{2}$

WANTED
Missing Fractions

Number Patterns in Additions

Investigating and exploring number patterns is an important part of algebra.

Have fun with these different types of number patterns.

Triangle patterns

Find the total of each TRIANGLE pattern. What do you notice?

1	2	3	4	5	6	7	8	9
1	2	3	4	5	6	7	8	
1	2	3	4	5	6	7		
1	2	3	4	5	6			
1	2	3	4	5				
1	2	3	4					
1	2	3						
1	2							
+1								

9	8	7	6	5	4	3	2	1
	8	7	6	5	4	3	2	1
		7	6	5	4	3	2	1
			6	5	4	3	2	1
				5	4	3	2	1
					4	3	2	1
						3	2	1
							2	1
+								1

Palindromes

Palindromes are numbers which read the same forwards and backwards.

44   121   7667   14541   492294

Which is the largest palindrome under 1000?

Write a 3-digit number.   329
Reverse it and add.   + 923
                              ————
                              1252
Repeat this until you get   + 2521
a palindrome answer.   ————
                              3773

Try with different 3-digit numbers.
Do you always get a palindrome?

Odds and evens

Which kind of number do you get if you add:

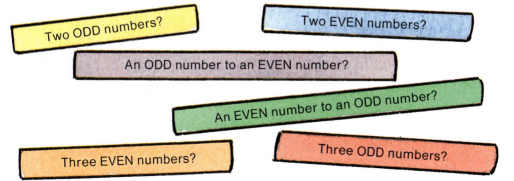

Two ODD numbers?

Two EVEN numbers?

An ODD number to an EVEN number?

An EVEN number to an ODD number?

Three EVEN numbers?

Three ODD numbers?

Mental additions

Numbers can be broken up into smaller units which give the same total:

$$46 = 40 + 6$$
$$= 30 + 16$$
$$= 20 + 26$$
etc

$$145 = 100 + 40 + 5$$
$$= 100 + 20 + 20 + 5$$
$$= 50 + 50 + 40 + 5$$
etc

We can use this fact to help us add up in our heads.

$$56 + 32 = 50 + 6 \ + \ 30 + 2$$
$$= 80 + 8$$
$$= 88$$

Try to add these up in your head:

54 + 25   31 + 48   62 + 28   58 + 52   63 + 75

Adding with money

Adding skills are needed when handling money.
Use your adding skills to find the answers to these tricky money problems. The money we use is the Drat and Petro. There are 100 petros (p) to a Drat (D)

Coin totals

Which totals up to 20p can be made using these coins.
A coin may not be used more than once.

Five coin totals

Add coins to make totals up to D1.
Which totals need more than FIVE coins to make them?

Coin game

A game for two players.
Use 10p and 20p coins.

Decide who will go first.
Take turns to place a 10p or a 20p coin on
the grid.
The first player to make a line which
totals 50p wins.
The line can be horizontal, vertical or
diagonal.

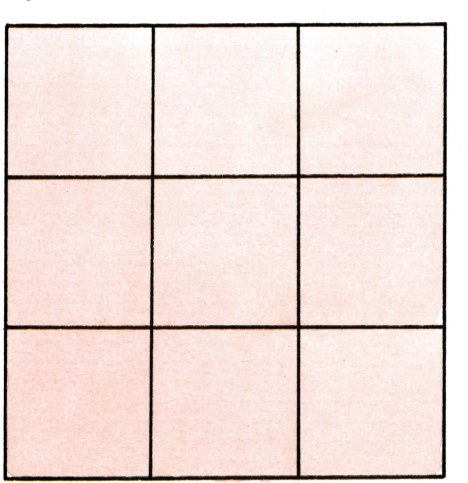

Adding with measures

Adding skills need to be used when we are measuring length, weight, capacity, and time.

How heavy?

The weights used to find the mass (weight) of each parcel are shown. How heavy is each parcel?

Weigh some objects of your own.

Finding perimeters

Perimeter is the distance measured all the way round a shape. Find the perimeters of these shapes:

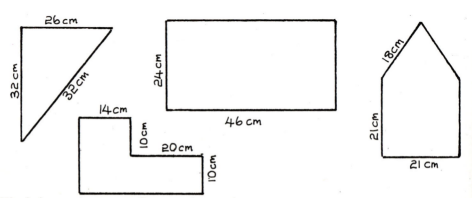

Find the perimeters of some shapes in your room.

26

Extra time

Look at each watch. What will the time be 45 minutes later?

Metric totals

Find the totals of these metric measures.

1.45m, 2.75m

1.850Kg, 2.560Kg

3.700 litres, 2.125 litres

6.5Km, 5.9Km

45mm, 69mm, 38mm

69ml, 36ml, 78ml

Imperial totals

Find the totals of these imperial measures.

11ins, 9ins, 6ins

12oz, 14oz, 13oz

6pts, 7pts, 5pts

12lb, 13lb, 9lb

6ft, 17ft, 21ft

9gal, 23gal, 12gal

Adding and data handling

Information is presented to us in all sorts of ways:

Graphs
Lists
Diagrams
Tables
Charts
Pictures

Use your skills to interpret the graphs and find the answers.

The graph shows average hours

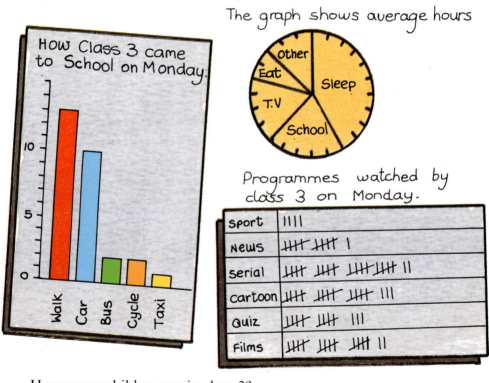

How Class 3 came to School on Monday.

Programmes watched by class 3 on Monday.

Sport	IIII
News	JHT JHT I
serial	JHT JHT JHT JHT II
cartoon	JHT JHT JHT III
Quiz	JHT JHT III
Films	JHT JHT JHT II

How many children are in class 3?

What is the average number of hours class 3 were awake?

How many children arrive at school under their own steam?

How many children watched films on Monday?

On average how many hours of TV were watched?

Glossary

Consecutive numbers These are numbers which follow on from each other e.g. 10, 11, 12 and 56, 57, 58, 59

Digits The digits are: 0, 1, 2, 3, 4, 5, 6, 7, 8, 9
Some numbers have two digits (35, 78, 95)
Some numbers have three digits (108, 567, 856)

Even numbers Numbers which can be divided exactly by two.
Here are some even numbers: 2, 6, 18, 74, 90, 142

Imperial measures Units used for measuring. The common ones still being used are:
Capacity – Pints (pts)   Gallons (gals)
Length   – Yard (yds)   Feet (ft)   Inches (ins)
Weight   – Ounces (oz)   Pounds (lb)

Magic squares Numbers arranged in a square grid. Each row, column and diagonal total is the same.

16	3	2	13
5	10	11	8
9	6	7	12
4	15	14	1

Each row, column and diagonal totals 34.
It is a magic square.

Odd numbers Numbers which cannot be divided by two without leaving a remainder.
Here are some add numbers: 3, 5, 27, 41, 89, 125

Palindromes Words and numbers which read the same when written forwards or backwards.
Here are some palindromes: MUM, DEED, 565, 2882

Perimeter This is the distance measured all the way around a shape.

Square numbers A square number is obtained by multiplying a number by itself.
36 is a square number because $6 \times 6 = 36$
81 is a square number because $9 \times 9 = 81$

Sum To sum a set of numbers means to add them together.
The sum of 12, 20 and 34 is 66.

Answers

Page 4:

Magic squares

4	3	8
9	5	1
2	7	6

8	1	6
3	5	7
4	9	2

Totalling score
34

Page 5:

Addition walls

29

14	15

6	8	7

1	5	3	4

55

24	31

11	13	18

6	5	8	10

2	4	1	7	3

A possible answer

21

10	11

6	4	7

5	1	3	4

Page 8:

Consecutive sums
You cannot make 2, 4, 8, 16, 32 by
adding consecutive sums.
15 can be found in more than one way:
$7+8$ and $1+2+3+4+5$.
Did you find any more?

Page 9:

Make a table showing light bars
needed to make each digit:

Digit	0	1	2	3	4	5	6	7	8	9
Light bars	6	2	5	5	4	5	6	4	7	6

Dice totals
With one dice each number should
have the same chance of turning up.
With two dice the total most likely to
turn up is 7.

Page 10:

Alphabet code
Germany

Word sum puzzle

```
   480        8943
 + 855      +   53
 ─────      ──────
  1335        8996
```

Page 11:

Addition square puzzle

5	+	4	+	6	=	15
+	■	+	■	+	■	+
6	+	3	+	2	=	11
+	■	+	■	+	■	+
4	+	5	+	5	=	14
=	■	=	■	=	■	=
15	+	12	+	13	=	40

Word total puzzles
Bee is only worth 12.
Turkey is worth 100.
How did you do?

Page 13:

Consecutive numbers
$573 = 286 + 287$ $905 = 452 + 453$
$759 = 379 + 380$ $399 = 199 + 200$
$439 = 219 + 220$ $733 = 366 + 367$

All digit adds
There are many possible answers.
Here are 2 more:

```
   243         782
 + 675       + 154
 ─────       ─────
   918         936
```

Page 14:

Addition grids

+	5	7	9	11
2	7	9	11	13
4	9	11	13	15
9	14	16	18	20
10	15	17	19	21
12	17	19	21	23

Problems grids
There are several
answers. Here are two

6	1
2	3

5	2
3	2

Page 15:

Trangle grids
A possible answer

```
    1
 7  2  3
 8  5  4
    6
```

Page 16:

Dice problem
Opposite faces of a dice total 7.
16 spots; 23 spots; 23 spots.

Word problem
660 stamps

Mental problems
Half; three quarters;
one whole

Page 17:

Digit problem
A possible answer

Page 20:

Simple equations
$8 + 9 = 17$ $15 + 9 = 24$ $13 + 12 = 25$

Open equations

$0 + 10 = 10$	$0 + 3 = 3$	$7 + 0 + 13 + 20$
$1 + 9 = 10$	$1 + 3 = 4$	$7 + 1 + 12 = 20$
$2 + 8 = 10$	$2 + 3 = 5$	$7 + 2 + 11 = 20$
$3 + 7 = 10$	$3 + 3 = 6$	$7 + 3 + 10 = 20$
$\vdots$	$\vdots$	$\vdots$
$10 + 0 = 10$	Etc.	$7 + 13 + 0 = 20$

Additions sums

```
   43        56        38
 + 28      + 98      + 28
 ----      ----      ----
   71       154        66
```

Page 21:

Addition grids

+	4	5
3	7	8
6	10	11

Word problems
14 & 11
5

Addition sequence
45, 50, 55, 60, 65, 70, 75, 80
34, 38, 42, 46, 50, 54, 58, 62,
30, 37, 44, 51, 58, 65, 72, 79

Missing fractions
quarter
three-quarters
three-quarters

Page 22:

Triangle patterns
Each total is 1083676269

Palindromes
999
Most 3-digit numbers will result in
palindromes when reversed and added.
One exception is 196.

Page 23:

Odds and evens
$0 + 0 = E$ $E + E = E$ $0 + E = 0$
$E + 0 = 0$ $E + E + E = E$ $0 + 0 + 0 = 0$

Mental additons
79; 79; 90; 110; 138

31

Page 24:

Coin totals
All totals except 4p, 9p, 14p & 19p can
be made.

Five coin totals
88p, 89p, 98p & 99p

Coin problem
The minimum is 3p, the maximum
£1.50

Page 26:

How heavy?
1.800Kg (1800g); 650g; 280g

Finding perimeters
90cm; 140cm; 99cm; 108cm

Page 27

Extra time
8·48; 12·10; 8·35; 4·55; 16·30

Metric addition
4.20m; 4.410Kg; 5.825 litre
12.4km; 152mm; 183ml

Imperial addition
26ins; 39oz; 18pts
34lb; 44ft; 44gal

Page 28

Adding and data handling
28 children; 14 hours; 15 children
(13 walk and 2 cycle) 17 children;
4 hours

Index

Answers   30
Calculator   9, 17, 18, 19
Codes   10
Coins   24, 25
Consecutive   6, 8, 13
Data   28
Dice   7, 9, 13, 16
Digits   5, 13, 15, 17, 19, 20
Digit cards   5, 6
Equations   20
Even numbers   23
Fractions   16, 21
Games   4, 6, 7, 13, 19, 25
Glossary   29
Graphs   28
Grids   4, 11, 12, 14, 15, 21, 25
Investigations   5, 8, 9, 14, 15, 17, 18,
   19, 22, 24
Length   26
Magic squares   4, 12

Measures   26, 27
Mental   16, 21, 23
Missing numbers   4, 5, 11, 14, 15, 17,
   20, 21
Money   24, 25
Number cards   5, 6, 8
Odd numbers   15, 23
Palindromes   22
Patterns   4, 8, 12, 15, 21, 22, 23
Perimeters   26
Practice   4, 26, 27
Problems   5, 10, 11, 13, 14, 15, 17, 18,
   19, 20, 21, 24, 28
Probability   9
Puzzles   10, 11
Sequences   21
Square numbers   8
Time   27
Weight   26

Adding squares

5	+		+	1	=	10
+		+		+		+
1	+	3	+		=	6
+		+		+		+
	+	5	+	5	=	
=		=		=		=
10	+		+	8	=	

3	+		+	5	=	12
+		+		+		+
2	+	5	+		=	14
+		+		+		+
	+	2	+	5	=	
=		=		=		=
9	+		+	17	=	

Calculator Maths

Get a calculator and work out these sums.

Add up the ages of all the boys in the class.

_____

Add up the ages of all the girls in the class.

_____

Add up the numbers of this week's dates.

_____

Ask 4 children in the class to tell you a big number, but not bigger than 100, then add them up. ☐ + ☐ + ☐ + ☐ =

An adding grid.

Finish this adding grid.

+	8	5	10	3	6	1	2	9	4	7
6										
3							5			
10		15		13						
5					6					
2										
9			19							
0										7
7		12								
8				11			10			
1										
4										

How many times did you get 12? ☐
How many times did you get 15? ☐
How many times did you get 20? ☐

Calculator Maths

Get a calculator and do these sums with it.

Count how many chairs in the class and work out how many legs they have. _____

Ask the big children in class the size of their shoes, then add up the numbers they tell you.
_____

If you know how old your Mum, Dad and brothers and sisters are add up their ages. _____

Look at the cars in the car park and add up the numbers.
_____

Playing Cards. with 4 people.

Get a pack of playing cards.
Use only cards 2 to 9.
Share out the cards.
Each person lays out a card.
Take turns to put a card on
the line and make it
add up to 11.

Like this:

$5+6=11$

$5+3+3=11$

Get 2 dice

Shake the dice and make 3 sums from the 2 numbers you shake.

Like this:

$$3 + 4 = 7$$
$$3 \times 4 = 12$$
$$4 - 3 = 1$$

Throw the dice 6 times and Write down the sums you make.

Write the numbers 11 to 20 in the boxes below.

11									20

Add 2 numbers next to each other, write down the sum.

11 + 12 =
12 + 13 =

Number codes.

A	B	C	D	E	F	G	H	I	J	K	L	M
1	2	3	4	5	6	7	8	9	10	11	12	13
N	O	P	Q	R	S	T	U	V	W	X	Y	Z
14	15	16	17	18	19	20	21	22	23	24	25	26

DOG is 4+15+7=26   RED is 18+5+4= 27

CAT is

MAN is

GIRL is

BOY is

BLUE is

PINK is

ANT is

DEER is

TREE is

CAR is

BALL is

Dominoe Sums

Get the dominoes and turn 10 of them up-side-down. Pick up 2 of them and add up the spots, then make up a take away sum like this. Put the one with most spots first.

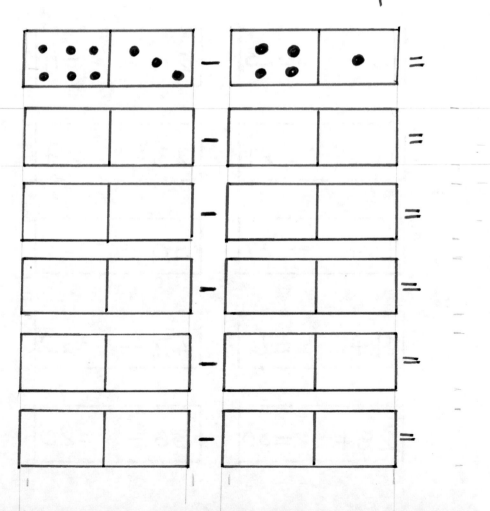

Finish these sums

7 + = 15	24 − = 12
26 + = 32	32 − = 25
14 + = 23	20 − = 11
15 + = 21	23 − = 9
13 + = 27	50 − = 21
9 + = 24	42 − = 22
28 + = 50	36 − = 20

Burst the bubble

Take a number from the first bubble and take away any number from the second bubble then find the answer in the third bubble.

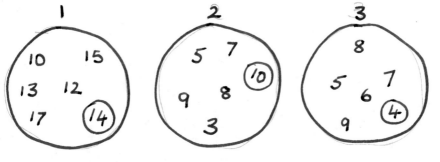

1

10   15
13   12
17   (14)

2

5   7
     (10)
9   8
   3

3

8

5   7
  6
9   (4)

like this.

14 − 10 = 4